THIS NATURE JOURNAL BELONGS TO:

....

D1736644

A NOTE TO PARENTS:

This nature journal contains prompts that are suitable for ages 4-14, but younger children will need an adult to help guide them through these nature exploration exercises. The prompts are designed as starting points for exploration, and can be adapted or added to, depending on your local environment.

Safety: Some of the explorations in nature involve cutting with knives, making fire or designing primitive weapons. All these sections are marked with a black bar at the bottom of the page, in their own section, and we recommend no matter how old the child is, all these tasks should be done with adult supervision. The Mulberry Journal takes no responsibility for how you conduct activities, and trusts you'll do so with safety and common sense.

Mulberry
PRINT CO.

More amazing home learning resources at
themulberryjournal.com

⊙ @mulberryjournal

This nature journal is inspired by Leo - our lionhearted young adventurer who teaches us daily to slow down and appreciate the unnoticed, luminous, extraordinary living things hiding in nature. Keep being curious, little love.

Mum & Dad (The Mulberry Journal Co-Founders)

MOVING AT A SNAIL'S PACE

Find a garden snail and track its speed. You'll need a timer or timer app on a phone and a ruler. If the snail is on concrete/brick, gently mark at the back of its tail with chalk. If on a leaf, mark with a pen. Time for 5 mins and then measure the back of its tail with another mark. Measure the distance between both marks. Multiply that distance by 12 and that will be the speed per hour. E.g If the snail moves 2 inches (5cm) in 5 mins, it will move 24 inches (60cm)/hour. Write your results below.

NATURE JOURNAL

NATURE GAMES

Choose your favorite game (eg. noughts and crosses/tic-tac-toe, chess) and try to re-create it with nature finds. You could use gumnuts, seed pods, leaves, sticks, bark and stones. You could also make up a game of your own. Write down the rules to your adapted or original game below.

THIRSTY PLANTS

Buy a box of the same type of seedlings and conduct a science experiment over a week. Leave one dry (the control in this experiment), pour water onto another, and other types of liquid - the same amount each time - onto the rest (eg. orange juice, coffee, tea, milk, soft drink/soda). Keep careful records below of each plant + what you observe about its form each day (eg. is it wilting/flaccid, or healthy/ turgid?) Do any plants die? Which liquid is the best 'food' for plants + why?

NATURE JOURNAL

BUILD A SHELTER THAT COULD KEEP YOU SAFE AND DRY

Collect sticks, large leaves and other materials, and build a shelter that could keep you safe and dry for a night outdoors. (Optional: actually sleep in it if the weather is warm enough!) Draw a picture or paste a photo of your shelter below.

NATURE JOURNAL

 ## LOOK WITH YOUR EARS

Step outside and close your eyes, or use a blindfold. Get your sibling, friend or adult to help you. Call out what you hear, and get your helper to write down every sound you hear over a period of a few minutes. After your blindfold is off, draw and label what you hear below. What was the faintest noise you heard?

NATURE JOURNAL

SET SAIL WITH RIVER BOATS

Make river boats using only natural materials. Find natural materials that float and put them together to build your own boat. Take your boats to a local creek or lagoon to test. Draw or plan your boat design below. How did your boats float?

ROCK POOL RUSH HOUR

Rock pools and tide pools can be busy little ecosystems. Because they're tidal and only exist at certain times of the day when the tide is lower, creatures who inhabit them are often bustling around, feeding and hunting in their small window of time, before the tide rises again. Go to a local coastal area at low tide and observe what's happening in a tide pool. How many creatures can you see? Draw them below.

NATURE JOURNAL

WHAT'S BROWN AND STICKY?

A stick! Find a stick in your backyard or a local reserve/park and brainstorm all the things you could use it for. Can you think of 20 uses for a stick? 50? Write your ideas down in a list below and draw diagrams if you like.

NATURE JOURNAL

 ## THERE'S SOMETHING IN THE WATER

Fill a shallow container or dish with water. Leave it in a bushy or forested area for a few days and then go back and study what/who's in it. Tally up the different animals, insects and natural elements (dirt etc.) below.

STUDY TRANSPIRATION

Tie a clear plastic bag around the leaves of a tree using tape. Leave in the sun for a few hours. Draw a picture of what happens in the bag.

NATURE JOURNAL

 ## MAKE PEBBLE MANDALA ARTWORKS

Collect pebbles or small round stones and make artworks by laying them on the ground. Research the origins of the mandala (Sanskrit for 'circle') and create your own mandala art from pebbles. Draw your design below.

NATURE JOURNAL

WHY CICADAS SHED THEIR SKIN

Collect cicada shells and draw what you find. Find out why cicadas shed their skin. Do they only do it once, or many times? Then research the skin shedding processes of other animals and insects too. Which other animals shed their skin?

NATURE JOURNAL

RECORD A NATURE SOUNDSCAPE
Use a smart phone or tablet app to record sounds (you may have to ask an adult to lend you their phone/tablet). Write down all the possible nature/outside sounds you could record below, then cross them off in your journal as you capture each sound. Edit into a soundscape using GarageBand app or another audio editing app.

NATURE JOURNAL

MAKE A NATURE DIORAMA

Use an old shoebox and collect nature finds to set up a nature scene. Print and stick a photo (or draw a picture) of your diorama below, and describe what's inside.

NATURE JOURNAL

 ## ALL THE VIBRANT COLORS OF NATURE

Collect leaves, flowers, sticks, bark, seed pods and anything else you can find in your local area to create a rainbow of nature finds. Draw a picture or stick your treasures here. How many colors are there?

NATURE JOURNAL

 ## OOOEY GOOEY SQUISHY MUD

Study the benefits of mud. Stand in a muddy spot in bare feet. Research and write down what mud is used for in indigenous cultures, construction and skin care.

NATURE JOURNAL

 ## MAKE YOUR OWN NATURAL PAINTS

Did you know you can make paints from natural things, like berries, rocks and bee pollen? Grind down rocks to a powder, or push softer plants and berries through a sieve. Add a little water to make paint. Blue – blackberries, blackcurrants, blueberries. Red – beetroot, rose petals, cranberries, strawberries. Yellow – mustard powder, pumpkin, bee pollen. Paint with your colors below.

DUCK DIETS - QUACK QUACK

Is it a good idea to give bread to ducks? Should people ever feed wild animals?
Design a poster educating your local community about why to avoid feeding ducks.

BECOME A FARMER - AN ANT FARMER!

Get an ant farm starter kit and research which ants to put in your ant farm. Draw a picture of the pattern that the ants make in their farm. Why do they do that?

NATURE JOURNAL

WHAT'S THAT IN LATIN?

All plants have common names (that most of us use) and scientific names, in a language called Latin. Scientific plant names help describe both the "genus" and "species" of plants in order to better categorize them. Choose some plants in your backyard or local area and do some research to find their scientific names. Draw a picture of the plant below and label it with its scientific name.

NATURE JOURNAL

SPINDLY SPIDER WEBS

Find 2-3 spider webs (you may need to do this over a few days) and draw them below. Are the patterns different? Do you know which spiders made those webs? How can you find out?

MAKE STICK CONSTRUCTIONS

Collect sticks and make stick constructions. Try making the tallest, widest, strongest structures. What can you make using only sticks? Draw a diagram of your favorite structure below.

NATURE JOURNAL

 DO A LEAF SIZE COMPARISON

Explore why different trees have different sized leaves. Find large and small leaves and compare the different sizes, shapes and features. Draw or trace them below.

NATURE JOURNAL

MAKE A DAM

Use natural found materials to make a dam without water in it. When you think
it's strong enough to hold, release water into your dam. Draw a diagram of your
dam and the materials you used. Record your results and observe why it did/didn't
work. How could you improve it so it's stronger next time?

CONSTRUCT A NATURAL DRAINAGE SYSTEM

Hunt in your local area for pieces of fallen bark (don't rip off trees, just collect from the ground). Use tape + string to connect pieces of bark together to make a drainage system. Test with water! Place a bucket at the bottom and pour from a jug of water at the top + watch the water run down. Draw your drainage system below.

NATURE JOURNAL

TOWERING ROCK STATUES

Make rock statues by balancing rocks on top of each other. Do the smallest or biggest need to go at the base? Draw and color your tower below.

NATURE JOURNAL

 ## FOLLOW A LOCAL DAM/RIVER TO WHERE IT MEETS THE OCEAN

Study the journey from where the river originates and follow it as far as you can (take an adult with you). Does it empty at the ocean? What kind of animals + habitats do you observe along the way? Draw a detailed map of your findings.

NATURE JOURNAL

PESKY PERENNIALS + WAYWARD WEEDS

What are the weeds growing in your local area? Research the origins of a particular weed. Where did it come from? Is it a native or introduced? Was it brought to control something else? Draw a picture of your findings and a short report below.

MAKE UP A DANCE TO THE SUN (OR A RAINDANCE)

Use your nature finds as part of your imaginary ceremony and make a dress up costume. Write down the lyrics to your song and draw/explain the choreography/actions for your dance moves.

YOUR NOCTURNAL NEIGHBORS

Study the nocturnal animals that only come out after dark in your area. Make a list and/or draw them below. What do these animals eat/hunt?

NATURE JOURNAL

 ## FOLLOW THE WEATHER PATTERNS IN YOUR LOCAL AREA

Use the internet to research the weather every day in your local area for a week.
Compare the forecast to the weather you observe outside. Is the forecast correct?
Make a 7-day bar graph to track temperatures each day below.

NATURE JOURNAL

MAKE A BARK ARTWORK OR 'BARKWORK'

Collect pieces of dry fallen bark (don't rip off trees, just collect from the ground).
Arange it below or on another sheet of paper or cardboard. Use glue to stick it
down, and add paint if you like. Take a photo of your art and print + paste it below.

NATURE JOURNAL

 ## WHAT DOES IT WEIGH?

Weigh your nature finds. What does each item weigh? Take a set of scales into the bushland or forest area nearby and categorize based on weight. List your nature finds from lightest to heaviest along with their weights.

NATURE JOURNAL

 ## DIGGING SOME DIRT

Ask your parent or caregiver if you can borrow a shovel. Take one shovel of earth.
Pull it apart and study what's in it. Report and draw what's in the dirt below.

NATURE JOURNAL

THE FRESHEST WATER YOU'LL EVER HAVE

If you know a storm or heavy rain is forecast, put out a clean container to catch rainwater. Draw a picture of your container + how much water you trapped. When it's dry, collect your water and pour yourself a cup. How does the water taste? Is it different to water from your tap or water filter? Write down your observations.

NATURE JOURNAL

COMPOST BUGS

Start a compost bin and study the bugs that are attracted to it. You might need to dig through gently with gloves or a little spade to see the worms and other creepy crawlies hiding. Draw the bugs you find below. Why are bugs important helpers for your compost bin? How do they help breakdown organic food scraps? Is there anything that shouldn't go in your compost bin?

NATURE JOURNAL

FROG FRIENDS (CROAK, CROAK)

Study amphibious animals (do you have any frogs in your area?) What sounds do they make at night? Do all frogs croak, or do some make other sounds? Make up a new species of frog. Draw it, color it in and describe its habitat.

NATURE JOURNAL

BECOME A BIRDER

Did you know a bird watcher is also called a 'Birder'? Go out and sit still in a variety of spaces (like in a park, forest or by the beach). Create a mindmap below of your locations and draw or describe the birds you saw in each location. Were they behaving differently?

BARK CANOES IN A STOP-MOTION FILM

Collect pieces of dry fallen bark (don't rip off trees, just collect from the ground). Make characters from sticks, leaves or gumnuts + place in the canoes. Use a camera or phone on a tripod to create a stop-motion film (you may need to Google how, or ask an adult how to do this). Storyboard your stop-motion film below.

NATURE JOURNAL

 WHAT'S HIDING IN SAND?

Next time you're at the beach, take a plastic bag and bring a cup or two of sand home. Pour the sand through a sieve. What is left? Draw or trace what you found in the sand. Do you know how sand is formed?

NATURE JOURNAL

SOMETHING FISHY

Learn about a fish local to your area (or state/region). Is it native or introduced?
What is its habitat and what does it eat? Does it migrate seasonally or to mate?
Draw a picture below and a map showing where this fish lives.

NATURE JOURNAL

 ## (LITERALLY) WATCH GRASS GROW

Measure grass over the course of a few weeks and document its progress.
Take a photo at the start and the end and stick the photos below (or draw before +
after pictures). Plot the observed growth rate of the grass in a graph below. Include
a description of any rainfall.

THE HILLS ARE ALIVE

Make instruments from things you find in nature. Hints: think percussion instruments that you can hit and bang, or dried seed pods you can rattle. You could make a woodwind instrument (a long hollow stick or shell that you can blow makes a simple flute!) Here's a challenge - can you make a stringed instrument?

NATURE JOURNAL

RE-CREATE PREHISTORIC TOOLS

Research pre-historic tools used by the first human species on earth. Can you re-create similar tools using things you find in nature nearby? Draw or stick in a picture of your tool/s below. Write a speech below talking about the history of the tool and how you made it (or you could even make a podcast episode!)

NATURE JOURNAL

MEET THE LOCALS

Learn about an animal or bird local to your area (or state/region). Is it native or introduced? What is its habitat and what does it eat? Does it migrate seasonally or to mate? Draw a picture below and a map of where this animal's habitats are.

NATURE JOURNAL

MAPPING - THEN & NOW

Find an old photo or map of your local area and compare it to a modern photo or map to see what has changed. To find an old photo or map, you can try your online library archives, or visit a local historical society or library. Make a copy or take a photo of the archives and stick it below. Write a list of what has changed.

NATURE JOURNAL

 BIRDS OF A FEATHER

Find a bird feather and do some research to identify the bird. Make sure you wash your hands thoroughly after picking up the feather. Make a pretend social media account (or a diary) for the bird below. Draw it a profile picture, note who its friends are, what it likes to eat + where it lives. You can include 'status updates' (or diary entries) of what the bird might do in a day.

NATURE JOURNAL

MAP YOUR AREA

What habitats and ecosystems exist in your local area? Make a map of your area and label/color all the natural areas (like parks, grasslands, beaches, forests and rivers/lakes).

TORNADO IN A BOTTLE

Fill one empty plastic soft drink/soda bottle 2/3 full with water, then place a metal or rubber washer on top. Place another empty bottle the same size on top so the bottle openings are facing each other with the washer in between. Use gaffa/duct tape to seal it all together. Flip then swirl the bottle around and see the tornado in a bottle! Time how long the tornado takes compared to just falling straight down.

NATURE JOURNAL

 ## HIGH TIDE & LOW TIDE

Study the tides in the ocean, local lake or lagoon/marshland and their effect on the waterway as a whole. Do man-made structures or uses of the land affect the tides or contribute to coastal erosion? Draw a magazine ad below warning people about the effects of coastal erosion in your local area.

NATURE JOURNAL

 ## TRUE COLORS

Collect some nature finds and sort into colors. Match each color to items in your house. Draw your nature find and its matching object below.

CREATE SHELL ART
Collect shells from your local beach or coastal area and use them to make an artwork in the sand. Take a photo and paste it below, or draw your artwork. Remember to leave the shells where you found them!

FLOWER PRESSING

Collect flowers in your yard or local area and use books or a flower press to flatten them. You will need to leave them 1-3 weeks so all the moisture drains away but the color remains. Stick the dried/pressed flowers below and label with their common and scientific names.

DOES IT SINK OR FLOAT?

Collect an array of nature finds and fill a container with water. Draw and write the name of each item below, and add two columns: Prediction | Result. Note your scientific prediction FIRST - whether you think it will sink or float. Then drop the nature item into the water and record the result in the next column. Did any results surprise you?

NATURE JOURNAL

BLOCKING OUT THE SUNLIGHT

Use sticky tape to cover a leaf on a tree with black paper on both sides for 7 days. It should go pale. Remove the paper after a week and leave the leaf in sunlight again for 7 days. What happens to the leaf? Trace your leaf onto the page below and draw a line down the middle. Color the left side of the page the pale leaf color, and the right side of the page the green leaf color.

LIGHTNING STRIKES

Plot the time intervals between lightning strikes during a storm and note down the time in between strikes below. Take photos using long exposure and paste them in, or draw pictures of the lightning strikes below.

SNOW MELT

If you live in an area with snow, collect some and place it inside your house. Track how long the snow takes to melt. When it has melted, you should have water. Is the water as clear as the water from your tap? Can you make a cup of tea using the 'snow water'? Why should you always boil water from nature before you drink it?

NATURE JOURNAL

THE ANTS GO MARCHING

Have you ever noticed ants marching up a wall or in your backyard? Follow the trail of ants with a magnifying glass to see where they go and what they are busy doing. Do they look calm and organized, or rushed and angry? Can you find their home - the ant nest - where the whole ant colony lives? Research the life cycle of an ant, and the social and communal behaviors of ant colonies - one of nature's marvels!

ODD FRUIT & VEGGIES

Find the most obscure fruit or vegetable in your local supermarket/grower's market. Is it local or imported? When is it in season? Learn about how to grow it and how to cook with it. Make a poster promoting the fruit/vegetable below.

NATURE JOURNAL

EGGS NEAR ME

Make a list of local animals in your area that lay eggs. Look up the egg sizes of each animal then draw them below and label them.

SAFETY NOTE!

THIS SECTION CONTAINS TASKS
THAT YOU'LL NEED ADULT HELP
AND SUPERVISION WITH!

NATURE JOURNAL

DISSECT A DEAD BUG - EWWW!

Ask an adult to help with this one. Find a dead bug and ask an adult to help you cut it carefully with a sharp knife. Draw a picture of your dissected bug below.

COMFY CATERPILLAR COCOONS

Ask an adult to help with this one. Gently catch caterpillars and study the cocoon process. Make them a comfy home first - you'll need holes for air, water and sticks and leaves for them to climb on + eat! Write down what you'll need for their enclosure. Draw a picture of the cocoon + type of butterfly/moth they are going to turn into. Release the butterflies/moths after they emerge.

IS IT EDIBLE?

Ask an adult to help with this one. Research what is naturally growing in your local area and what is edible and safe to eat (caution: do the research with your adult as some plants and berries can be poisonous or cause allergic reactions in humans.) Once you've found what is safe, go and collect some and eat a little. Find or create a recipe or tea using one of your edible finds and write your recipe below.

NATURE JOURNAL

ROCK OR SEA FOSSILS

Ask an adult to help with this one. Research whether there are any commonly known fossil sites in your local area. Maybe they are a bit further away, and you can do a day trip. Take your journal and draw the fossils you find. Describe the location you found them. Do you know how old they are, and how they formed? Optional: Make your own fossil by carving a design into a half a potato. Dip your fossil design in paint or ink, and stamp it below.

NATURE JOURNAL

STINKY STUFF

Ask an adult to help with this one. Find some animal droppings in your local area. Using plastic gloves and a mask/lab goggles, see what you find in the animal poop. Make sure to wash your hands thoroughly afterwards. Record what you find inside the poop. What does this animal eat?

NATURE JOURNAL

DATE: /   /

MAKE A HOME FOR A LIZARD OR INSECT

Ask an adult to help with this one. If you find a lizard or insect around your home and can trap it safely, you can observe its behavior for a little while. First, find a cardboard box or jar and make your lizard/insect a leafy place to rest with a dark hole for hiding (a toilet roll is great). Your animal home must have food + water, and holes for oxygen (if using a jar, place plastic wrap on the lid with a rubber band, and poke holes for air). Write down and draw pictures of what your insect does. Remember to release your little friend after a few hours.

MAKE A WINDSOCK

Ask an adult to help with this one. A windsock is a device that shows you which way the wind is blowing. To make your own, you'll need a toilet roll, pipe cleaner/string, scissors, glue and party streamers. Cut the party streamers into approx 7 inch (18cm) lengths. Glue them to the inside of the toilet paper roll. Poke two holes in the top, and attach the string or pipe cleaner to create a hanger. Decorate the toilet paper roll if you like. Hang the windsock outside. Draw pictures of your windsock below showing when the wind is strong and when it is gentle.

MAKE SURVIVAL WEAPONS

Ask an adult to help with this one. Imagine you're stranded on a desert island, and make weapons that could be used for hunting your dinner. DON'T actually test this and hurt animals - remember you have ample food in your fridge and don't need to hunt :) Draw your weapons below.

NATURE JOURNAL

 ## HOW TO MAKE FIRE

Ask an adult to help with this one. Research how the first humans created fire. Gather materials to make a fire without using matches, fire starters or a lighter. Write a description of how to create fire using only natural materials, and draw a picture/diagram. Were you successful? How long did it take?

NATURE JOURNAL

 ### BUSHFIRES IN NATURE

Ask an adult to help with this one. Research why naturally occurring bushfires (started by lightning strikes) are regenerative and important for the death + rebirth cycle of nature. If possible, visit a forest recently burned by fire and observe the regrowth. Draw a picture of what you observe.

PLANTS AS MEDICINE

Ask an adult to help with this one. Choose a plant either native to your country/area or commonly grown, and research all its medicinal and therapeutic uses (eg. lemon myrtle, aloe vera, tea tree, camomile or something else). Draw a picture below, and some illustrations of how it can be used and its benefits (in tea, in oils, extracts etc.)

BLANK NATURE JOURNAL PAGES:

TO DOCUMENT YOUR OWN NATURE EXPERIMENTS AND FASCINATING FINDS

NATURE JOURNAL

DATE: / /

NATURE JOURNAL

NATURE JOURNAL

DATE: / /

NATURE JOURNAL

NATURE JOURNAL

DATE: /   /

NATURE JOURNAL

DATE: / /

NATURE JOURNAL

NATURE JOURNAL

DATE: / /

NATURE JOURNAL

DATE: /   /

NATURE JOURNAL

DATE: / /

NATURE JOURNAL

DATE: /   /

NATURE JOURNAL

DATE: /   /

NATURE JOURNAL

DATE: /   /

NATURE JOURNAL

DATE: /   /

NATURE JOURNAL

NATURE JOURNAL

NATURE JOURNAL

DATE: /   /

NATURE JOURNAL

NATURE JOURNAL

DATE: /   /

NATURE JOURNAL

DATE: /   /

Mulberry
PRINT CO.

FOR MORE HOME LEARNING RESOURCES LIKE
THIS, DOWNLOAD OUR FREE DAY NOTES OR
WEEKLY PLANNER PRINTABLES:

themulberryjournal.com/free-stuff

Made in the USA
Las Vegas, NV
01 October 2021